THANKFUL ME

Loving and Learning from A to Z

Thankful for all that I have,
all that I do,
all that I see.

T.R. Merryfield

Balboa Press books may be ordered through booksellers or by contacting:

Balboa Press
A Division of Hay House
1663 Liberty Drive
Bloomington, IN 47403
www.balboapress.com
1 (877) 407-4847

Because of the dynamic nature of the Internet, any web addresses or links contained in this book may have changed since publication and may no longer be valid. The views expressed in this work are solely those of the author and do not necessarily reflect the views of the publisher, and the publisher hereby disclaims any responsibility for them.

Any people depicted in stock imagery provided by Thinkstock are models, and such images are being used for illustrative purposes only.
Certain stock imagery © Thinkstock.

ISBN: 978-1-5043-5492-9 (sc)
ISBN: 978-1-5043-5493-6 (e)

Library of Congress Control Number: 2016906981

Print information available on the last page.

Balboa Press rev. date: 08/11/2017

BALBOA
PRESS
A DIVISION OF HAY HOUSE

Remember to be

thankful

for all that you have, see and do.

Even when some things

don't feel so good to you.

You are always loved and cared for

every single day.

Remember to be thankful...

Love will always come your way.

Blankets for cuddling.

Bunnies and teddy bears.

Brownies and ice cream.

My birthday each year.

Cupcakes with sprinkles.

Crayons galore.

Hot chocolate and cookies.

Playful cats on the floor.

Dd

Love from my Daddy.

Days at the beach.

Big dogs and little dogs.

The dreams I will reach.

Eyes that I see with.

Ears so I can hear.

Little elves making toys

Delivered early morning every year!

Friends that I play with.

Family in my home.

Ketchup on French fries.

My favorite ice cream cone.

Hot dogs I hold

With my strong little hands.

Hats for my head.

My hair... so many strands.

Iguanas and igloos.

Great big icicles that hang.

Ideas that I think.

Playing inside with the gang.

Peanut butter and jelly.

The jeans that I wear.

Jumping high off the ground.

Silly jokes that I hear.

Kisses and hugs.

Flying kites in the sky.

Kittens to play with.

Kicking balls way up high.

Lots of love all around me.

Lunch every day.

Great legs that I run with.

Autumn leaves that blow away.

Mommy who loves me.

The moon shining bright.

Music I play.

Fun movie time late at night!

Oatmeal for breakfast.

Oranges so sweet.

Blue sky over the rainbow.

Old and new friends that I meet.

Pp

Puddles to splash in.

Purple sunsets on summer nights.

Puppies to play with.

Picnic cloths red and white.

Asking questions in class

For quizzes and tests.

Running quick through the schoolyard.

Quiet time when I rest.

Running inside on rainy days.

Watching for rainbows in the sky.

Picking roses from a bush

For Mom who made a raisin pie.

Snowfall in the winter.

Snowmen in the sun.

Cozy scarves to keep me warm.

School is closed... let's have fun!

Twinkling stars in the night sky.

Tickles under my chin.

Wiggly toes on my feet.

I love my tent... let's go in!

Wishes and daydreams.

Weekends that are fun.

Water at our summer home.

Windows warmed by the sun.

Xylophones

... such pretty sounds.

X's on tic-tac-toe.

Superheroes with X-ray vision.

X marks the spot...

ready, set, go!

Yy

Growing taller every year.

Front yards...

there's work to do!

The yellow bus that passes by.

Saying "please" and "I love you."

Zebra stripes that are fun to see.

Zippers that go up and down.

Taking class trips to the zoo.

Zzzzzz's

when bedtime comes around.

So many things to be thankful for

in every single way.

See if you can think of some more

today and every day.